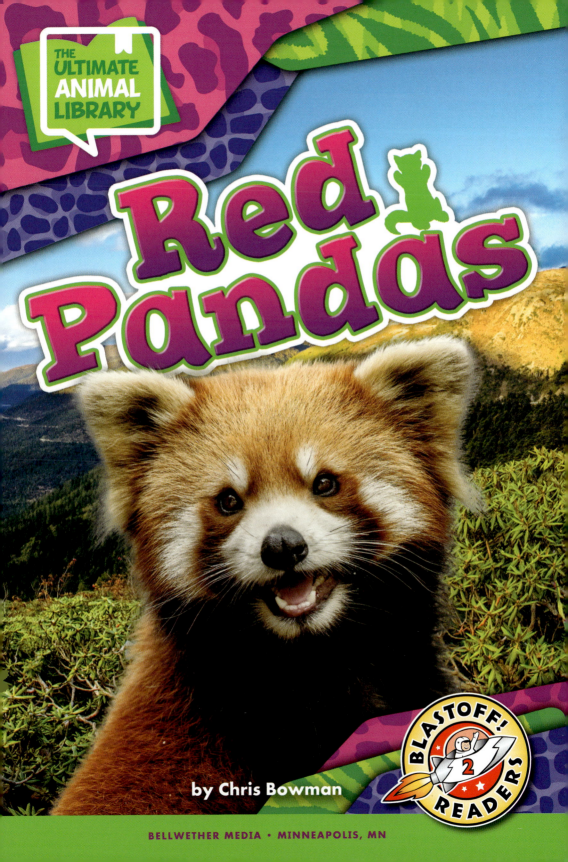

Blastoff! Readers are carefully developed by literacy experts to build reading stamina and move students toward fluency by combining standards-based content with developmentally appropriate text.

 Level 1 provides the most support through repetition of high-frequency words, light text, predictable sentence patterns, and strong visual support.

 Level 2 offers early readers a bit more challenge through varied sentences, increased text load, and text-supportive special features.

 Level 3 advances early-fluent readers toward fluency through increased text load, less reliance on photos, advancing concepts, longer sentences, and more complex special features.

★ **Blastoff! Universe**

Reading Level — Grade K → Grades 1–3 → Grade 4

This edition first published in 2026 by Bellwether Media, Inc.

No part of this publication may be reproduced in whole or in part without written permission of the publisher. For information regarding permission, write to Bellwether Media, Inc., Attention: Permissions Department, 3500 American Blvd W, Suite 150, Bloomington, MN 55431.

Library of Congress Cataloging-in-Publication Data

LC record for Red Pandas available at: https://lccn.loc.gov/2025003950

Text copyright © 2026 by Bellwether Media, Inc. BLASTOFF! READERS and associated logos are trademarks and/or registered trademarks of Bellwether Media, Inc. Bellwether Media is a division of FlutterBee Education Group.

Editor: Elizabeth Neuenfeldt   Series Designer: Veah Demmin

Printed in the United States of America, North Mankato, MN.

Table of Contents

What Are Red Pandas?	4
Cute Climbers	12
Growing Up	18
Glossary	22
To Learn More	23
Index	24

What Are Red Pandas?

Red pandas are **mammals** that live in the Himalayan Mountains. These animals grow to about 25 inches (63 centimeters) long.

Red Panda Report

Range

range = ▦

Status in the Wild

endangered

Habitat

forests

Red pandas have mostly red **coats**. Their bellies and legs are black.

coat

They have long **guard hairs**. Their **undercoats** are thick and soft.

Red pandas have long, furry tails. Their tails have stripes.

Their tails can grow up to 20 inches (51 centimeters) long.

Red pandas have round heads and short **snouts**. They have white markings on their faces.

They have large, pointed ears. They have small eyes.

snout

Cute Climbers

Red pandas live in mountain forests. They are strong climbers. Their tails help them **balance**.

They spend most of their time in trees. Red pandas usually live alone.

bamboo

Red pandas are most active at sunrise, sunset, and night.

These pandas are **omnivores**. They mostly eat bamboo leaves. They also eat berries and small animals.

Red pandas avoid **predators** such as jackals and snow leopards.

Their fur helps them hide among trees.

Growing Up

Female red pandas often make nests in trees. They have up to four **cubs** each spring or summer.

Red panda cubs stay in the nest for about three months.

cubs

nest

Cubs stay with their mother for about one year.

Then they go off to find their own food!

Life of a Red Panda

Name of Babies

 cubs

Number of Babies

 up to 4

Time Spent with Mom

about 1 year

Life Span

 up to 23 years

Glossary

balance—to stay upright

coats—fur or hair covering some animals

cubs—baby red pandas

guard hairs—long, thick hairs on the outside of a red panda's coat

mammals—warm-blooded animals that have backbones and feed their young milk

omnivores—animals that eat both plants and animals

predators—animals that hunt other animals for food

snouts—the noses and mouths of some animals

undercoats—layers of short, soft hair or fur that keep some animals warm

To Learn More

AT THE LIBRARY

Duling, Kaitlyn. *Red Pandas.* Minneapolis, Minn.: Bellwether Media, 2021.

Grack, Rachel. *Red Pandas.* Minneapolis, Minn.: Bellwether Media, 2024.

Sabelko, Rebecca. *Mountains.* Minneapolis, Minn.: Bellwether Media, 2022.

ON THE WEB

FACTSURFER

Factsurfer.com gives you a safe, fun way to find more information.

1. Go to www.factsurfer.com.

2. Enter "red pandas" into the search box and click 🔍.

3. Select your book cover to see a list of related content.

Index

bellies, 6
climbers, 12
coats, 6
colors, 6, 10
cubs, 18, 20
ears, 10
eyes, 10
females, 18
food, 14, 15, 21
furry, 8, 17
guard hairs, 7
heads, 10
hide, 17
Himalayan Mountains, 4, 12
legs, 6
life of a red panda, 21
mammals, 4
markings, 10
mother, 20
nests, 18, 19
night, 14

omnivores, 15
predators, 16
range, 4, 5
size, 4, 8, 9, 10
snouts, 10
spot a red panda, 11
spring, 18
status, 5
summer, 18
sunrise, 14
sunset, 14
tails, 8, 9, 12
trees, 13, 17, 18
undercoats, 7

The images in this book are reproduced through the courtesy of: Tao Jiang, cover (red panda); Almazoff, cover background, interior background; GooseFrol, cover (red panda icon); Eric Isselée, pp. 3, 23; Lubos Chlubny, p. 4; photoPepp, p. 6; Kieran, p. 7; XXD, p. 8; Hanjo Hellmann, p. 9; nyiragongo, p. 10; michaklootwijk, pp. 10-11; Robin, p. 11; Honza123, p. 12; wusuowei, p. 13; edfitzgerald, pp. 14-15; applezoomzoom, p. 15 (bamboo leaves); AB Photography, p. 15 (red panda, snow leopards); WildMedia, p. 15 (jackals); Hanna, p. 15 (berries); Ganga Raj Sunuwwar, p. 15 (small animals); Wildscotphotos/ Alamy, p. 16; Joe Blossom/ Alamy, p. 17; slowmotiongli, p. 18; BackyardBest/ Alamy, pp. 18-19; China News Service/ Getty Images, p. 20; havranka, p. 21.